Early Reading Intervention

**Part 1**

# Student Activity Book 1

## D'Nealian Edition

**PEARSON**

Scott
Foresman

scottforesman.com

**Editorial Offices:** Glenview, Illinois • Parsippany, New Jersey • New York, New York
**Sales Offices:** Boston, Massachusetts • Duluth, Georgia • Glenview, Illinois
Coppell, Texas • Sacramento, California • Mesa, Arizona

ISBN: 0-328-26054-1

# Table of Contents

Name _____

## Writer's Warm-Up

𝓂    𝓂

𝓂    𝓂

# Letter Cross-Out

Name _____

## Writer's Warm-Up

$m$    $m$

$m$    $m$

Activity 4

7

# Letter Cross-Out

Activity 6

Name _____

## Writer's Warm-Up

$m$   $m$

$m$   $m$

Activity 4

9

Name _____

## First Sounds

*m*

Activity 6

10

Name _____

## Writer's Warm-Up

$p$  $p$

$p$  $p$  •  •  |  •  •

$m$  •

**Lesson**
**4**

# First Sounds

$p$

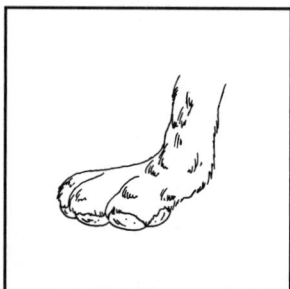

Name _____

## Writer's Warm-Up

$p$   $p$

$p$   $p$   •----•   |   •----•

$m$   •

## Letter Cross-Out

p m m
p m p
p m
m m p
p

Activity 7

Name _____

# Writer's Warm-Up

*p*   *p*

*p*   *p*

*m*

Activity 5

15

# Letter Race

m

p

Activity 7

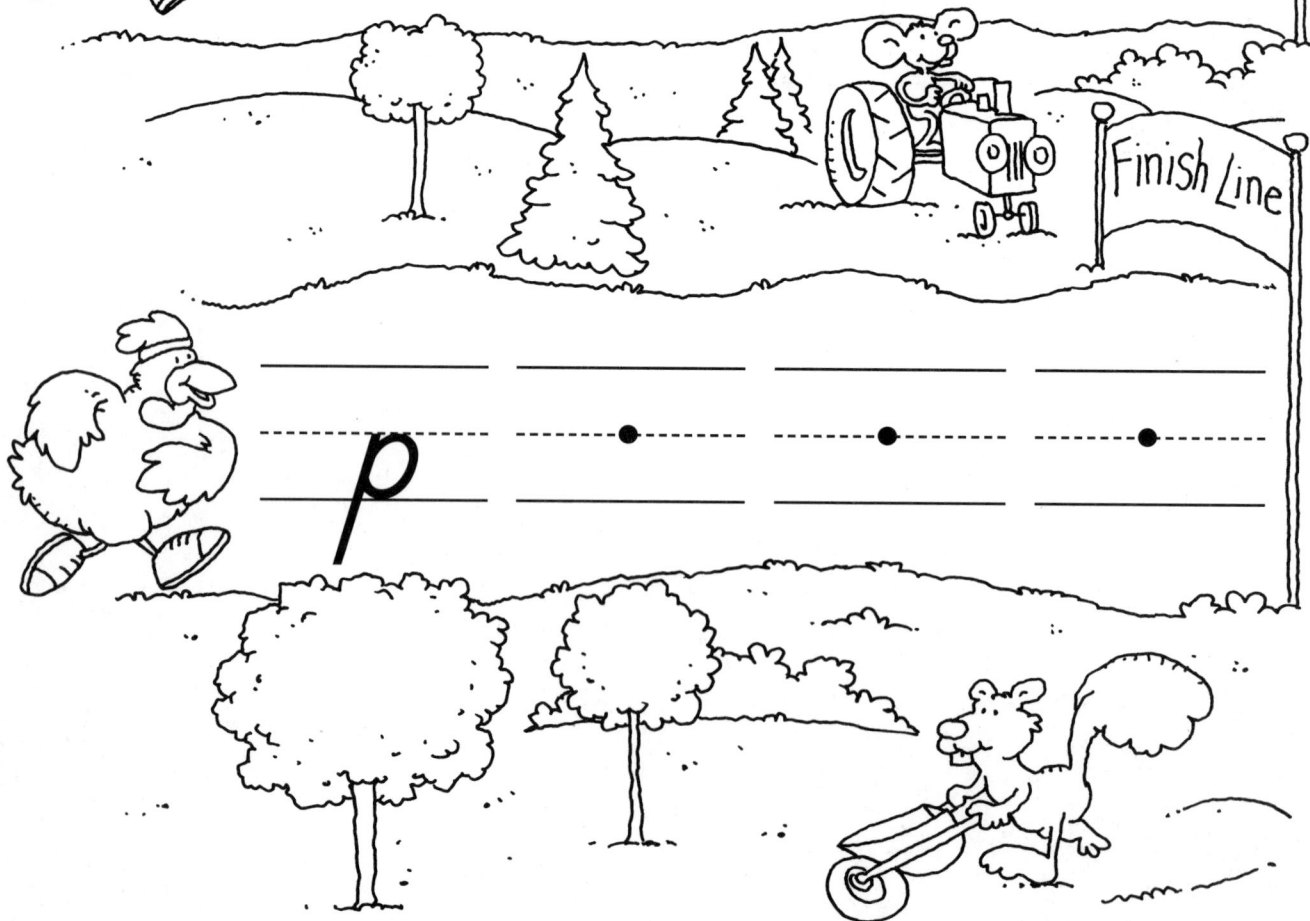

Name _____

## Writer's Warm-Up

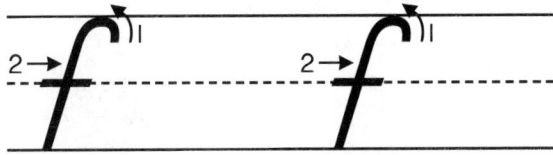

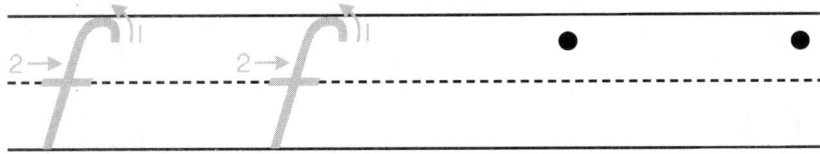   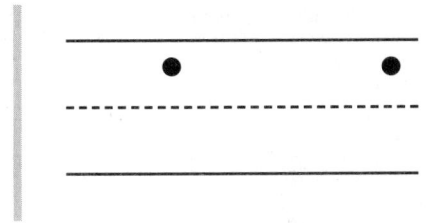

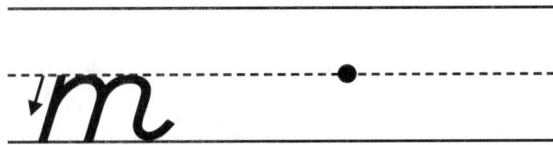

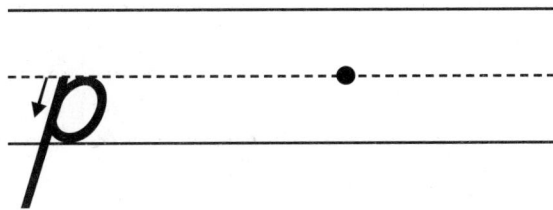

Activity 5

Name _____

# Letter Tag

 m
♥
p

p
m

p

m

m
p

p
m
★

m
p

18    Activity 7

Name _____

## Writer's Warm-Up

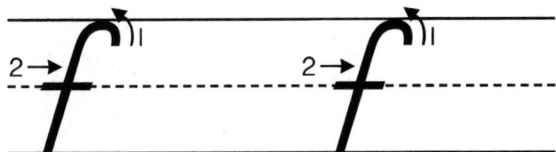

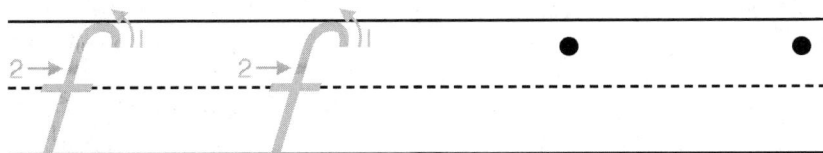 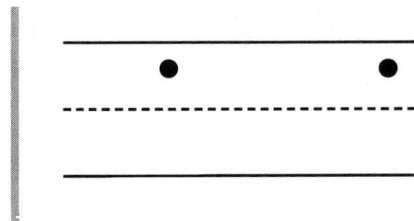

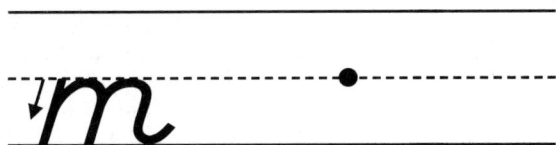

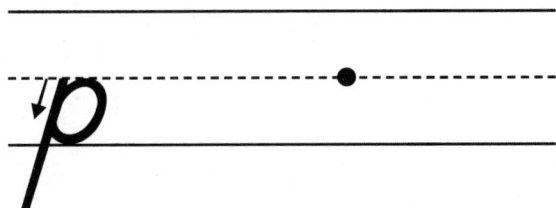

**Letter Writing Game**

$m$      $p$      $f$

Activity 7

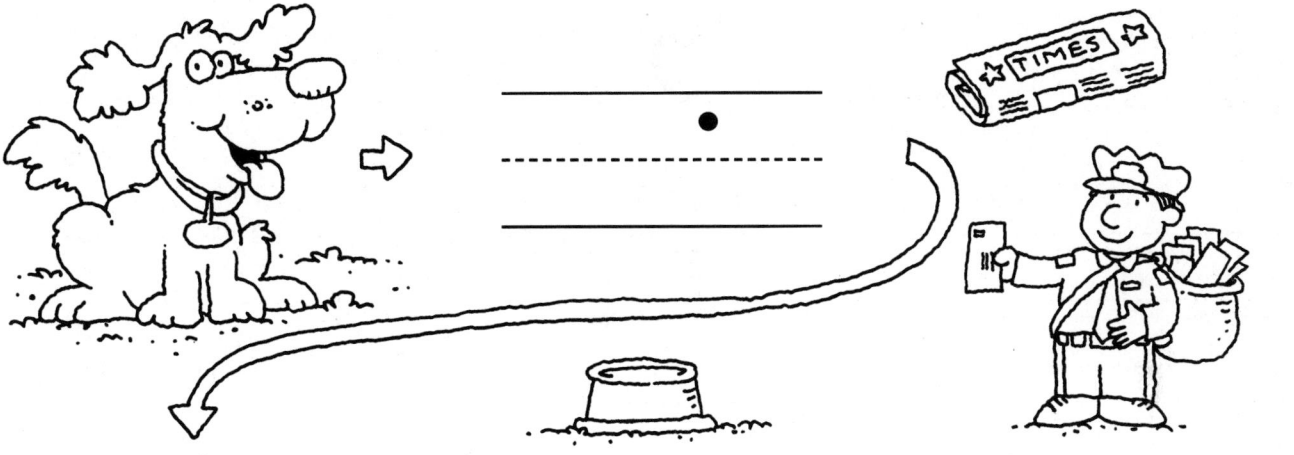

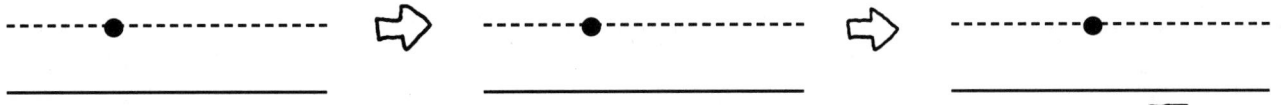

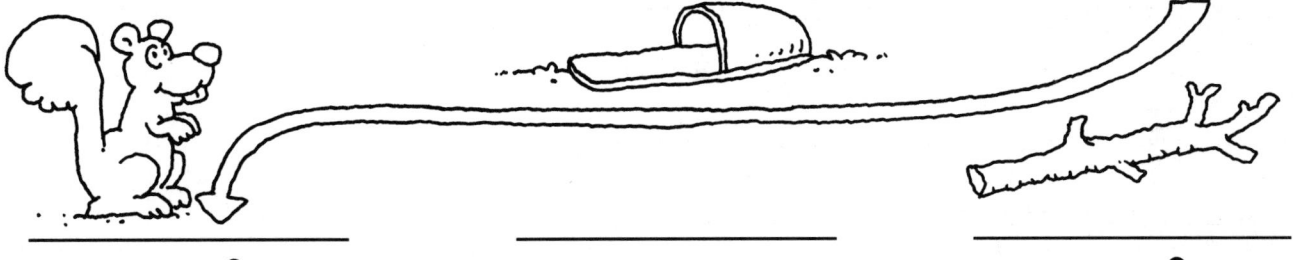

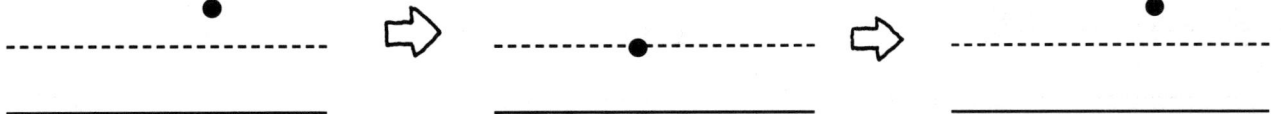

Name _____

# Letter Mission

Name _____

## Writer's Warm-Up

$c$     $c$

$c$     $c$     •     •          •          •

$m$          •

$p$          •

$f$          •

© Pearson Education, Inc.

Activity 5

22

Name _____

**Writer's Warm-Up**

$\mathcal{C}$          $\mathcal{C}$

$\mathcal{c}$     $\mathcal{c}$     •     •     |     •     •

$\mathcal{m}$     •

$\mathcal{p}$     •

2→ $\mathcal{f}$     •

Activity 5

23

**First Sounds**

*m p f c*

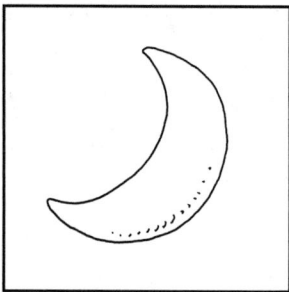

_____

- - - - - - •- - - - - - - - -

_____

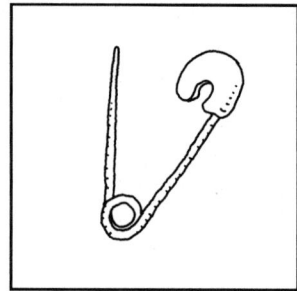

_____

- - - - - - •- - - - - - - - -

_____

_____

- - - - - - •- - - - - - - - -

_____

_____

- - - - •- - - - - - - - - -

_____

_____

- - - - - - •- - - - - - - - -

_____

Name _____

**Letter Cross-Out**

Activity 7

25

Name _____

## Writer's Warm-Up

$t$    $t$

$t$    $t$ •   •    •   •

$p$ •

$m$ •

$c$ •

$f$ •

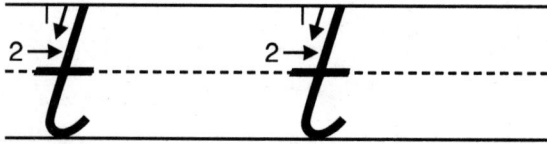

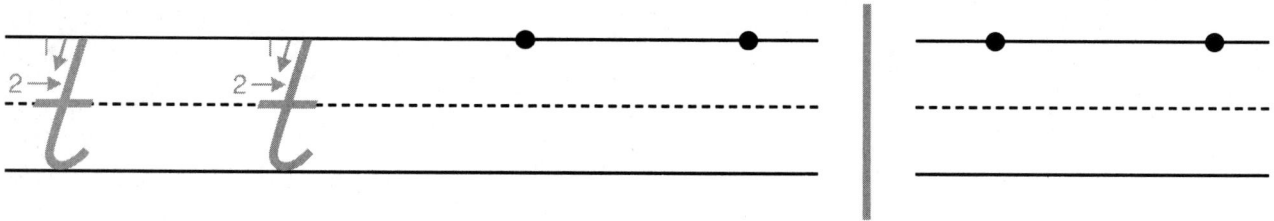

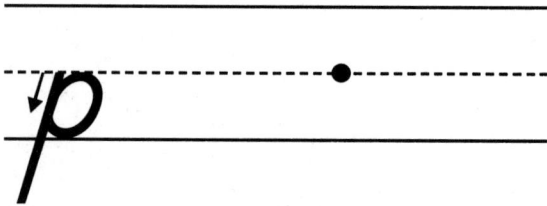

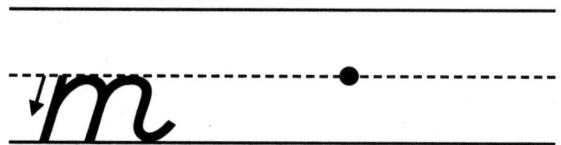

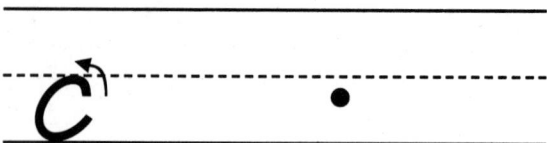

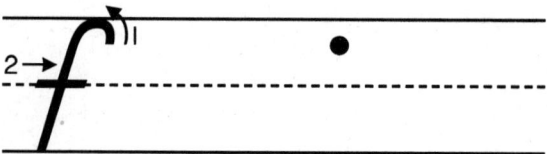

© Pearson Education, Inc.

Activity 5

26

Name _____

## Letter Race

$c$

Finish Line

$f$

Finish Line

$p$

Finish Line

$m$

Finish Line

Activity 7

27

Name _____

## Writer's Warm-Up

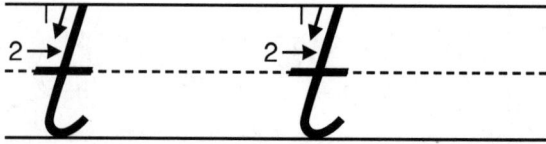

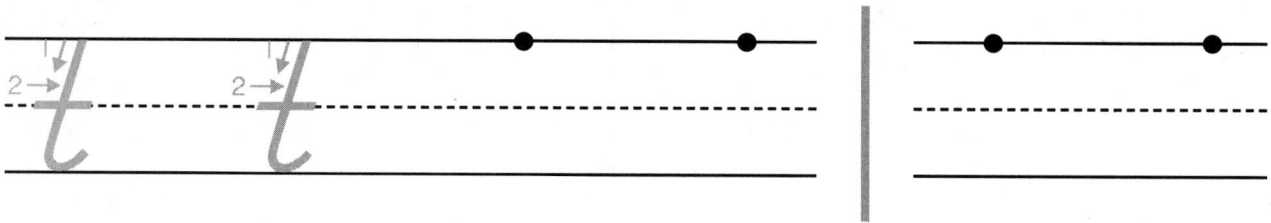

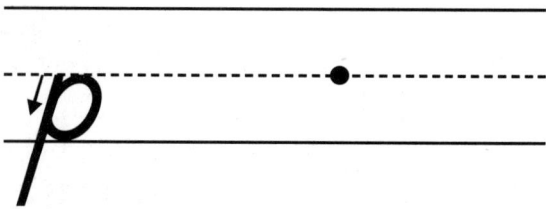

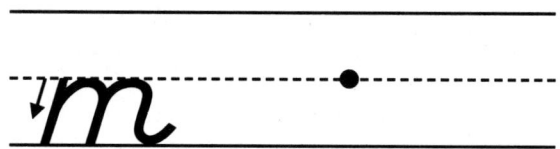

28

Activity 5

Name _____

## Letter Tag

 t
c
f

 p
f
c

 c
t
p

 p
m
c

 t
c
m

 f
p
m

Activity 7

 29

# Letter Mission

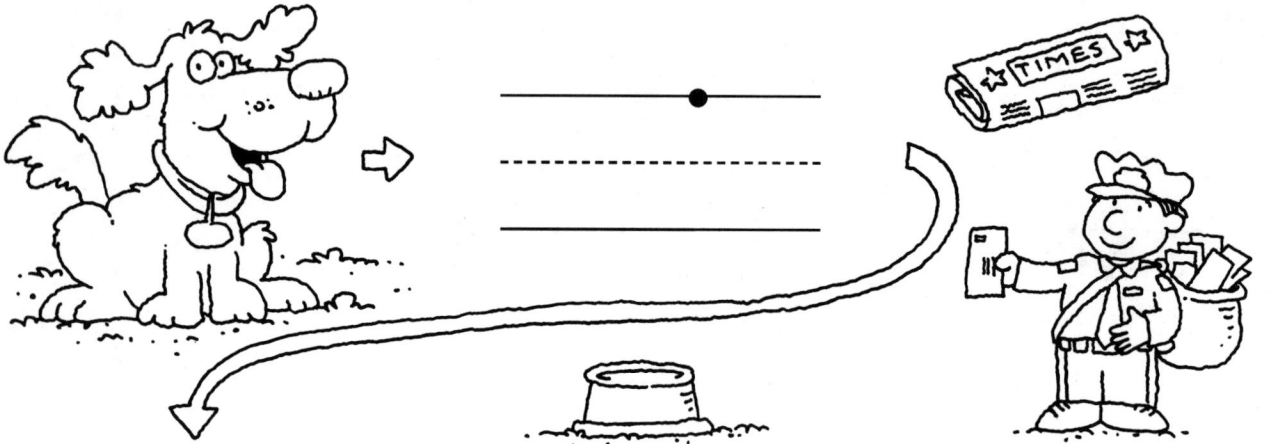

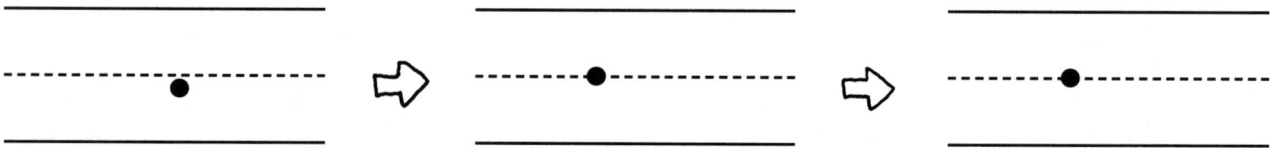

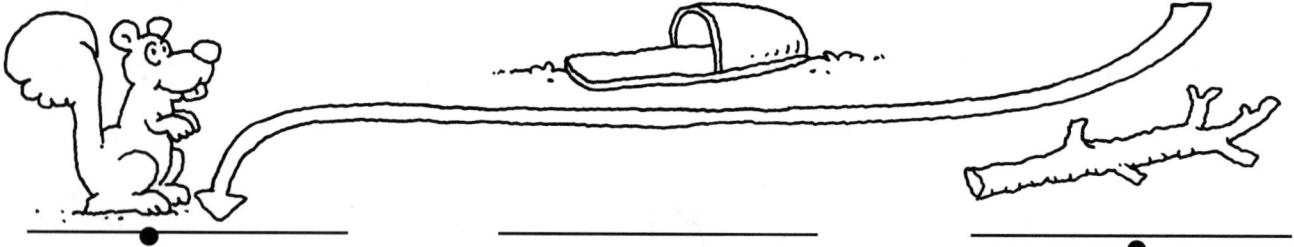

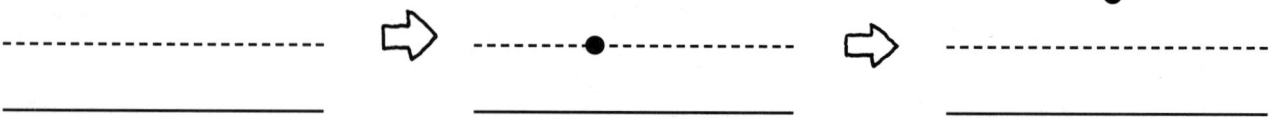

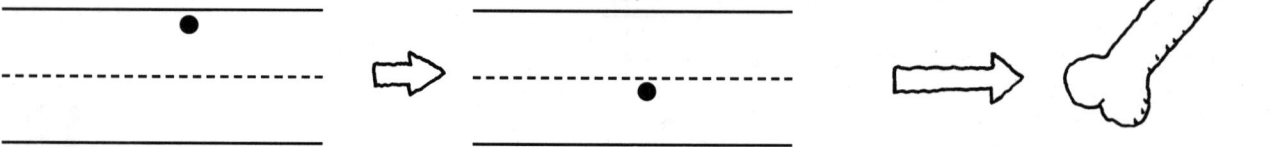

# Letter Writing Game

*t*

*c*

*f*

*p*

*m*

## Writer's Warm-Up

$s$ ↑     $s$ ↑

$s$ ↑     $s$ ↑     ●     ●          ●     ●

2→ $f$ ↑ ‖          ●               ↑ $m$          ●

$c$ ↑          ●               ↓ $t$          ●
                          2→ $t$

↑ $p$          ●

© Pearson Education, Inc.

Activity 5

## Writer's Warm-Up

$s$  $s$

$s$  $s$  •  •  |  •  •

$f$  •

$m$  •

$c$  •

$t$  •

$p$  •

33

Name _____

# First Sounds

*s t c f m*

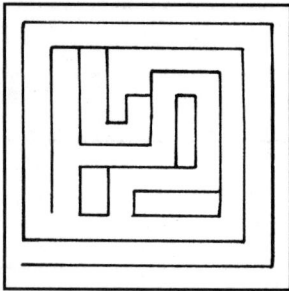

_____

- - - - - - • - - - - - - -

_____

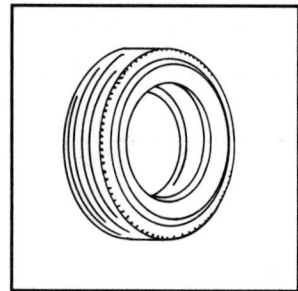

- - - - - - - • - - - - - - -

_____

- - - - - - - - • - - - - - - - - -

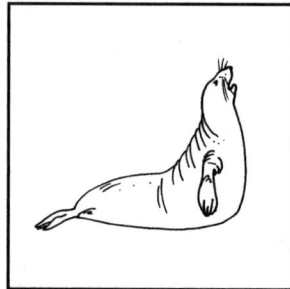

_____

- - - - - - - • - - - - - - - -

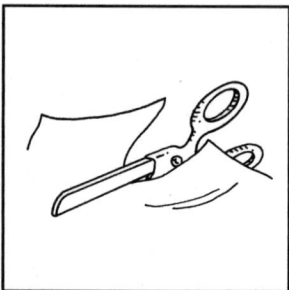

_____

- - - - - - • - - - - - -

_____

_____

- - - - - - • - - - - - -

_____

© Pearson Education, Inc.

Activity 7

Name _____

## Writer's Warm-Up

𝑑   𝑑

𝑑   𝑑

2→ 𝑓

𝑠

𝑝

2→ 𝑡

𝑚

𝑐

Activity 5

35

## Letter Cross-Out

t    p    s

f    c    t

s    p    f

c

Activity 7

Name _____

## Writer's Warm-Up

$d$   $d$

$d$   $d$   •   •      •   •

$f$   •        $s$   •

$p$   •        $t$   •

$m$   •

$c$   •

Activity 5

37

# Letter Race

Finish Line

*d*

Finish Line

*s*

Finish Line

*t*

Finish Line

*c*

Activity 7

# Name _____

## Letter Mission

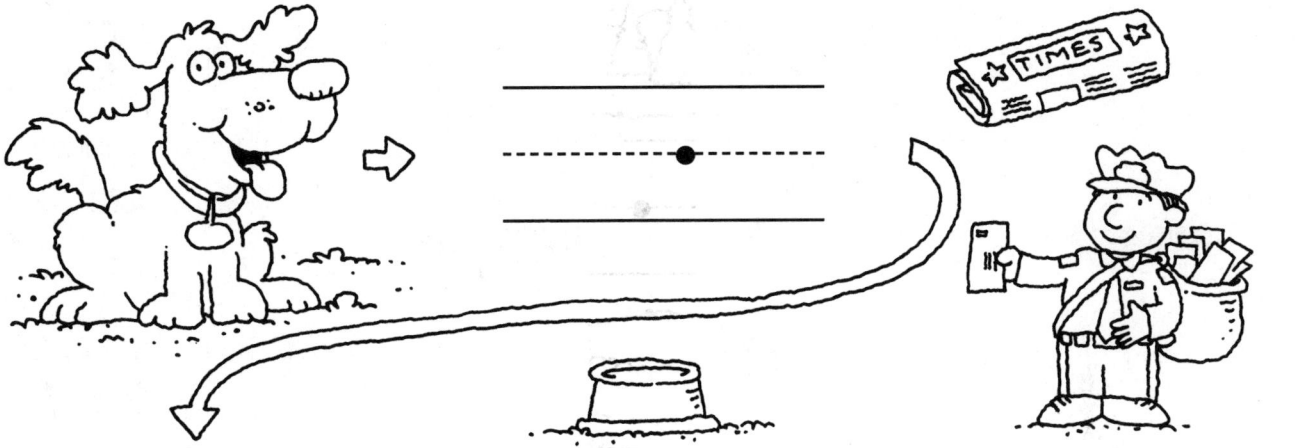

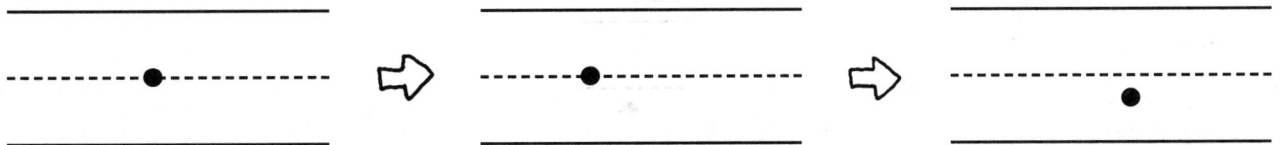

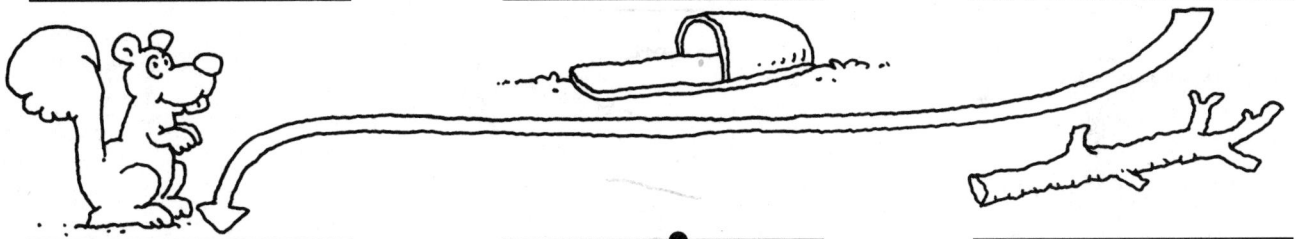

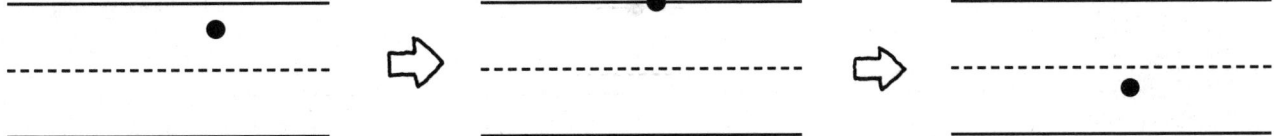

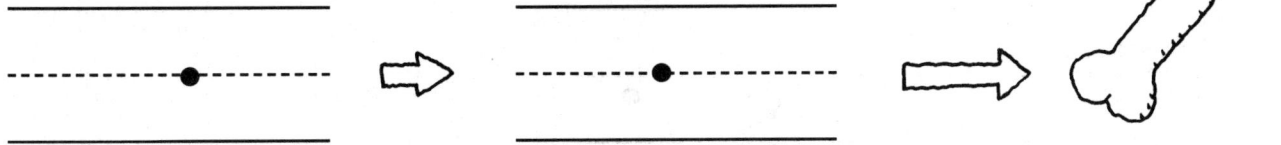

Name _____

## Letter Tag

 d
s
t

→ c
f
m

 m
s
c

→ t
m
d

→ f
c
s

→ m
d
t

 **Activity 7**

40

Name _____

## Writer's Warm-Up

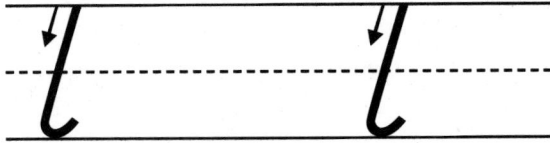

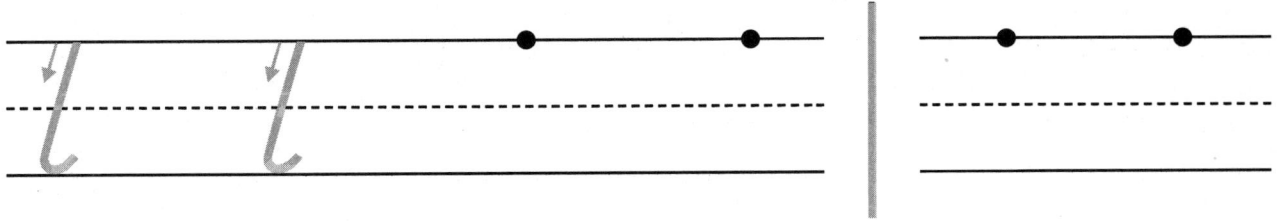

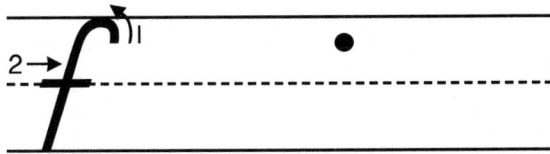

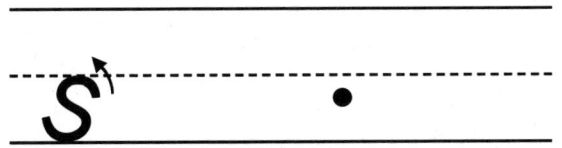

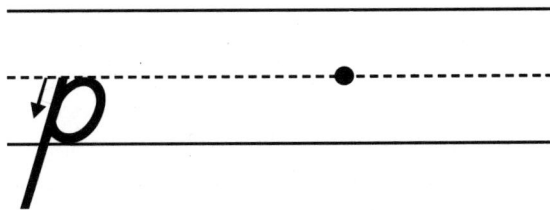

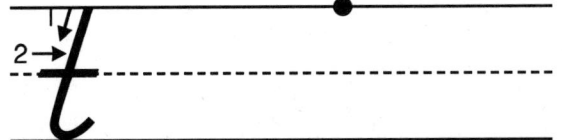

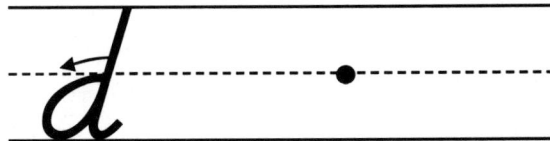

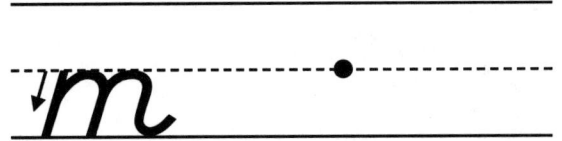

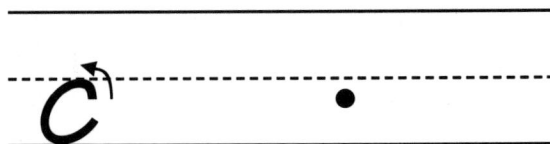

Activity 5

# Letter Writing Game

*t*

*p*

*c*

*d*

*m*

*s*

Name _____

**Writer's Warm-Up**

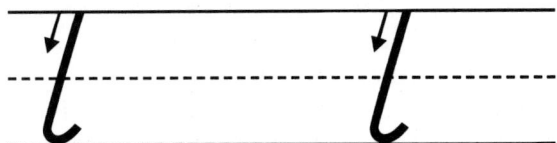

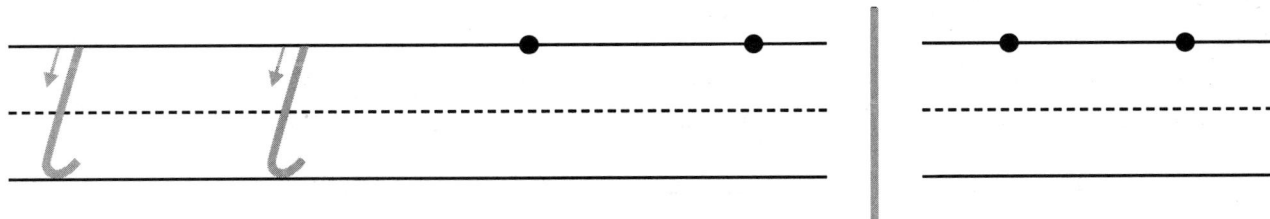

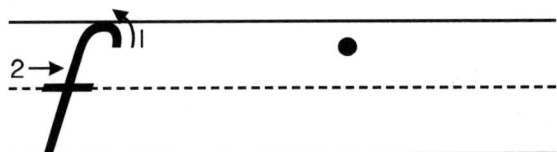

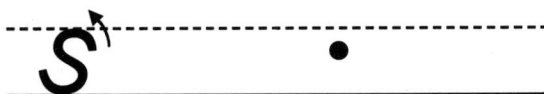

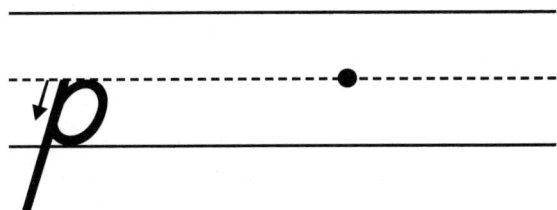

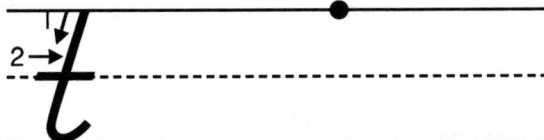

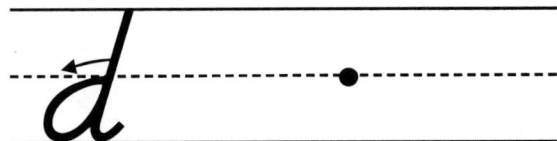

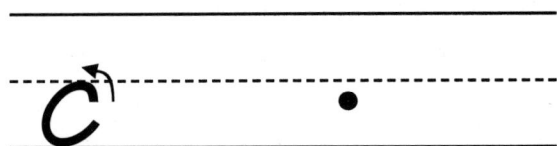

Activity 5

43

# Writer's Warm-Up

*a*    *a*

*a*    *a*

*f*    *s*

*d*    *t*

*l*

*c*

Name _____

## First Sounds

$l\ d\ s\ t\ p$

● 

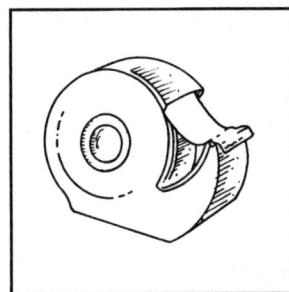

● 

● 

● 

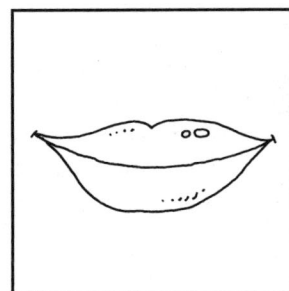

●

## Writer's Warm-Up

*a*   *a*

*a*   *a*

*f*   *s*

*d*   *t*

*l*

*c*

---

Activity 5

46

Name _____

## Letter Cross-Out

# Letter Mission

Activity 5

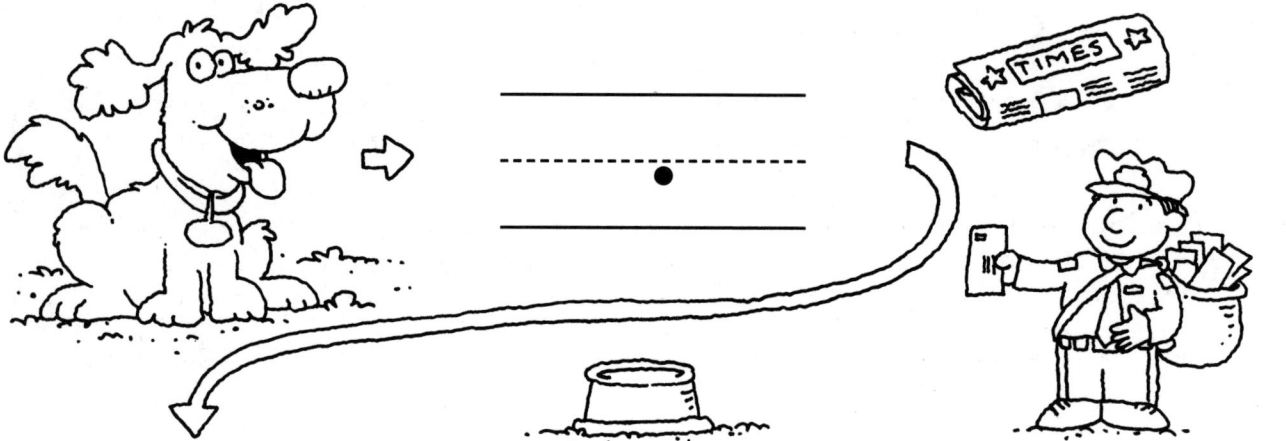

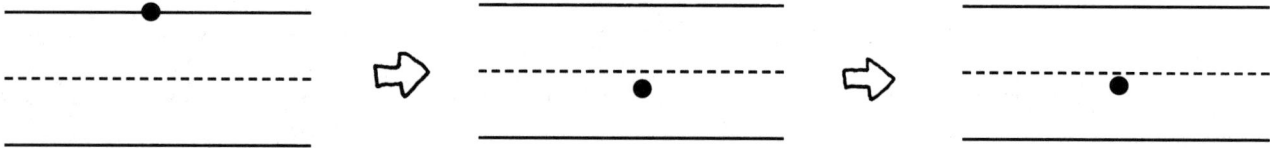

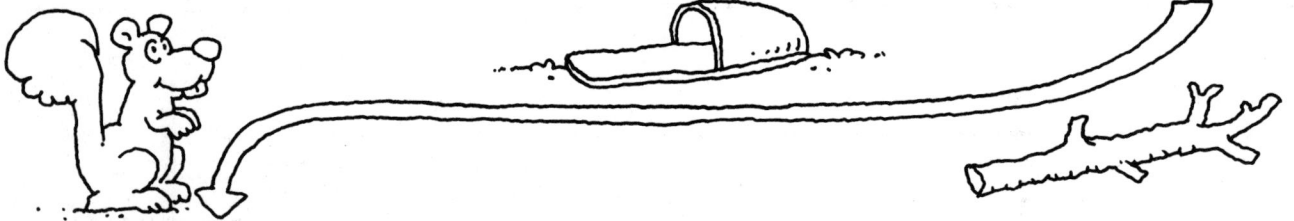

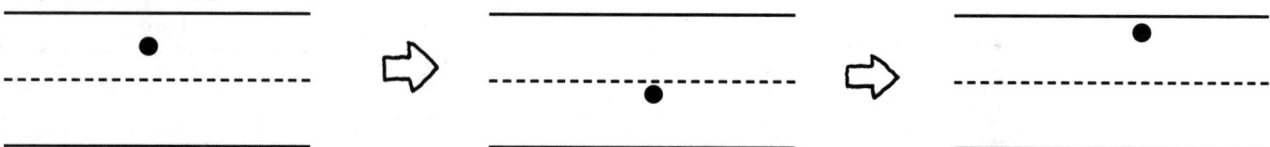

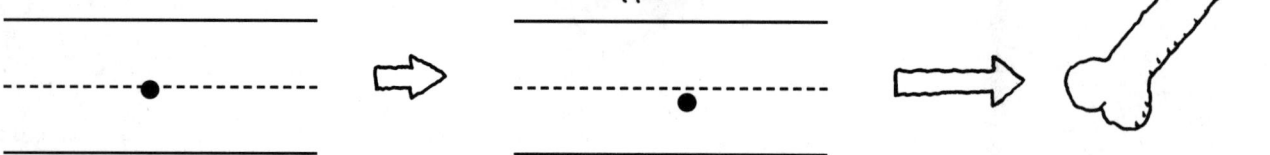

© Pearson Education, Inc.

Name _____

## Letter Race

$l$

$a$

$s$

$d$

Finish Line

Finish Line

Finish Line

Finish Line

49

Name _____

# Writer's Warm-Up

**Lesson**

**28**

*p*

*c*

*f*

*m*

*l*

*s*

*t*

*a*

*d*

Activity 5

50

**Letter Tag**

→ a
l
d

→ s
f
m

→ m
a
l

→ d
s
a

→ s
d
m

→ f
a
l

Name _____

## Letter Writing Game

*l*          *s*          *c*

*a*          *t*          *d*

© Pearson Education, Inc.

Activity 7

## Letter Mission

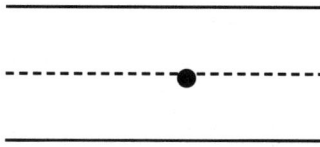

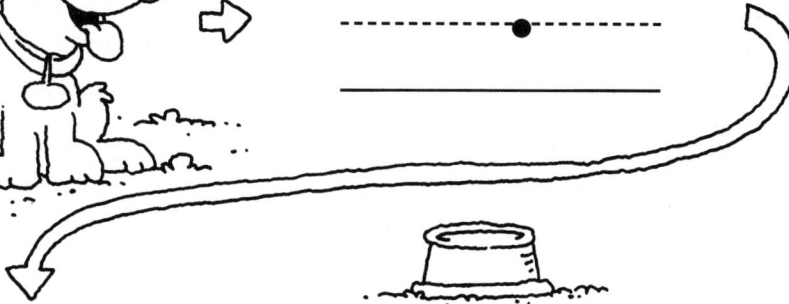

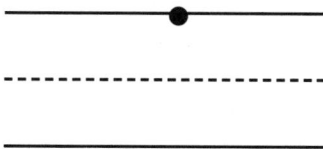
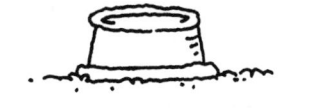
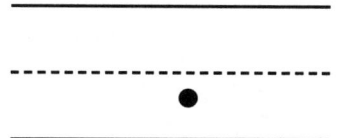

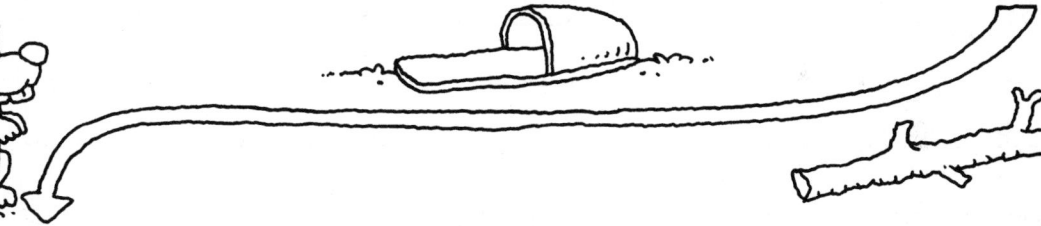

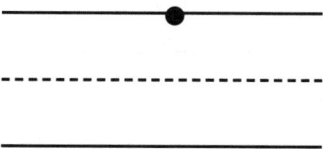
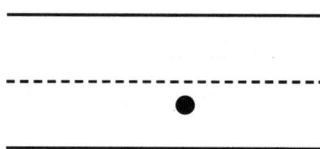
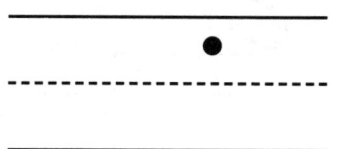

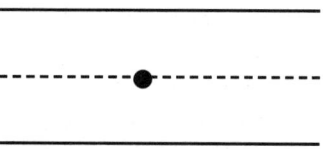
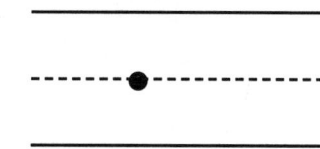

Name _____

**Writer's Warm-Up**

_O_     _O_

_O_     _O_     •     •  |  •     •

_a_     •        _s_     •

_d_     •        _t_     •

_l_     •        _c_     •

Activity 5

54

## Letter Cross-Out

Name _____

## Writer's Warm-Up

$\overset{\rightarrow}{O}$      $\overset{\rightarrow}{O}$

$\overset{\rightarrow}{O}$      $\overset{\rightarrow}{O}$

$a$

$d$

$l$

$s$

$t$

$c$

Activity 5

56

## Tic-Tac-Toe

| p | l | f |
|---|---|---|
| s | t | c |
| m | d | s |

| f | s | d |
|---|---|---|
| l | c | t |
| t | p | a |

| c | t | m |
|---|---|---|
| p | l | s |
| t | f | d |

# Letter Race

*l*

*d*

*t*

*p*

Name _____

## Writer's Warm-Up

*p*

*c*

*f*     2→

*m*

*l*

*t*     2→

*a*

*d*

*o*

*s*

Activity 5

59

## Writer's Warm-Up

*p*          •                    2→ *t*          •

*c*          •                    *a*          •

2→ *f*          •                    *d*          •

*m*          •                    *o*          •

*l*          •                    *s*          •

Activity 5

Name _____

## Tic-Tac-Toe

| p | l | f |
|---|---|---|
| s | t | c |
| m | d | s |

| f | s | d |
|---|---|---|
| l | c | t |
| t | p | a |

| c | t | m |
|---|---|---|
| p | l | s |
| t | f | d |

Activity 7

# Letter Mission

Activity 5

Name _____

## Letter Writing Game

_l_      _s_      _t_

_p_      _m_

Activity 7

63

Name _____

## Writer's Warm-Up

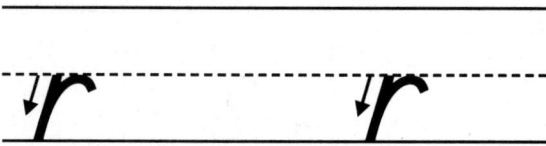

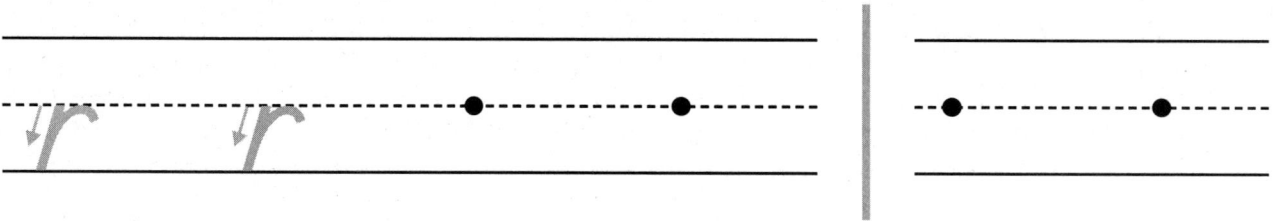

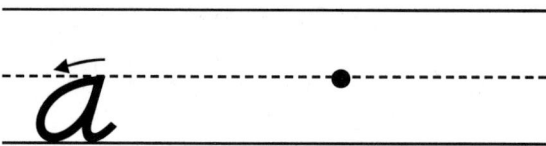

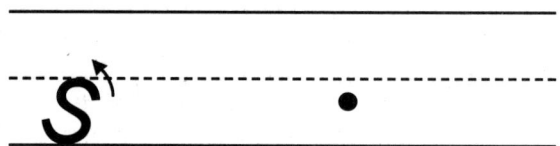

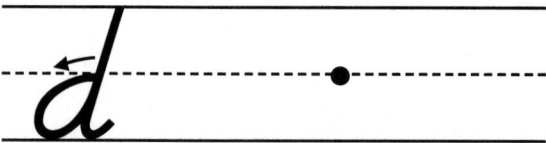

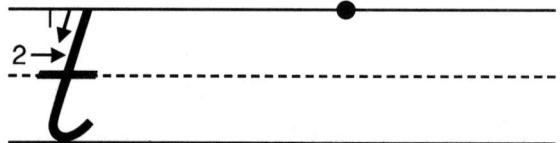

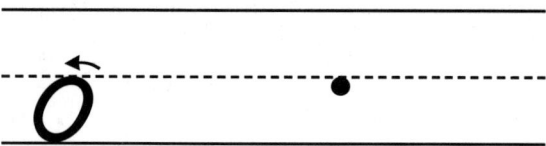

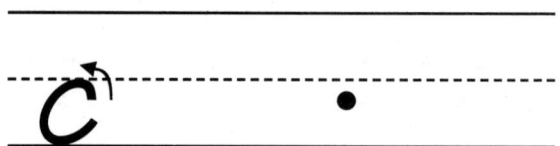

Activity 5

64

Name _____

# First and Last Sounds

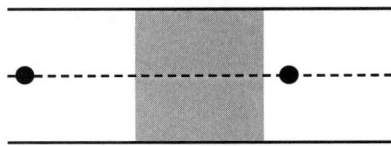

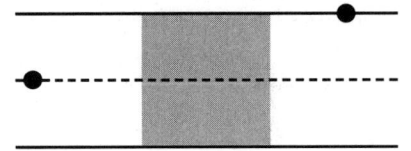

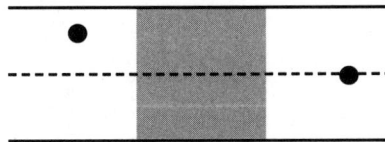

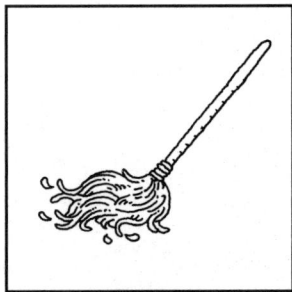

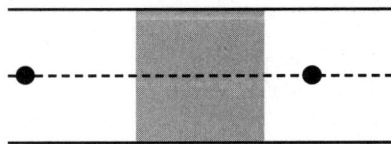

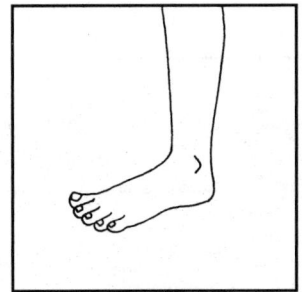

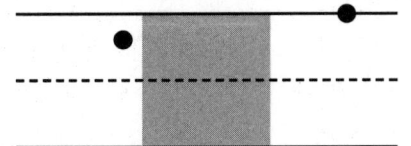

Name _____

## Writer's Warm-Up

*r*        *r*

*r*        *r*

*a*              *s*

*d*              2→ *t*

*o*

*c*

Activity 5

66

Name _____

## Tic-Tac-Toe

**1**

| | | |
|---|---|---|
| p | | s |
| l | | p |
| m | | m |

**4**

| | | |
|---|---|---|
| s | | t |
| f | | l |
| d | | m |

**2**

| | | |
|---|---|---|
| l | | p |
| c | | t |
| t | | d |

**5**

| | | |
|---|---|---|
| d | | t |
| c | | l |
| s | | p |

**3**

| | | |
|---|---|---|
| m | | t |
| s | | l |
| f | | s |

**6**

| | | |
|---|---|---|
| c | | p |
| t | | l |
| m | | f |

Activity 7

# Word Writing Game

Activity 7

Name _____

## Writer's Warm-Up

p

t

c

a

f

d

m

o

r

s

l

Activity 5

69

Name _____

# Word Maze

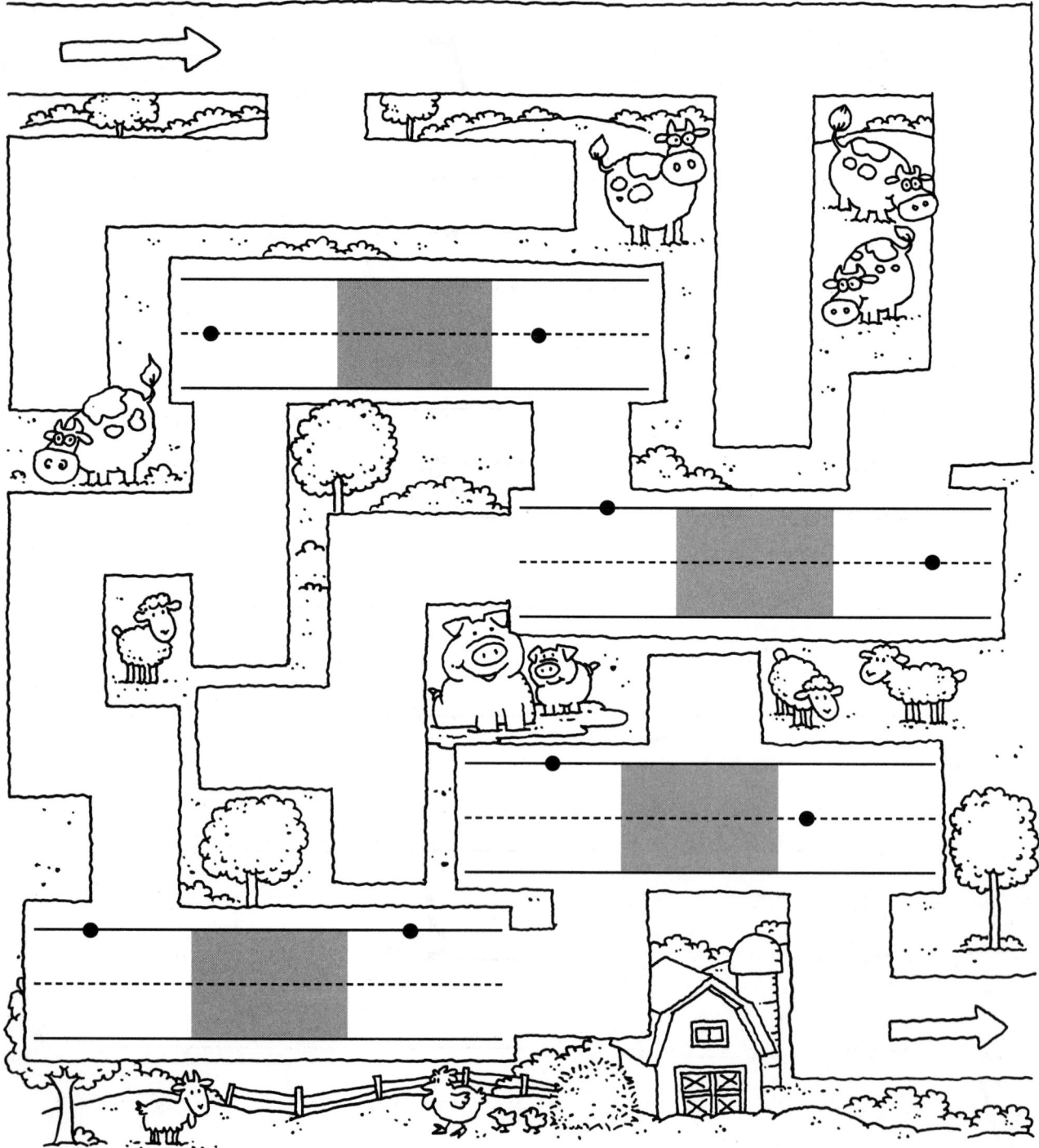

© Pearson Education, Inc.

Activity 7

Name _____

## Writer's Warm-Up

*p*   *t*   *m*   *o*

*a*   *l*   *d*   *f*

*c*   *s*   *d*   *o*

Activity 5

71

Name _____

## Letter Tag

 l
m
p

 s
t
f

 t
f
c

 p
l
m

 p
s
t

 l
s
t

Activity 7

72

# Treasure Hunt

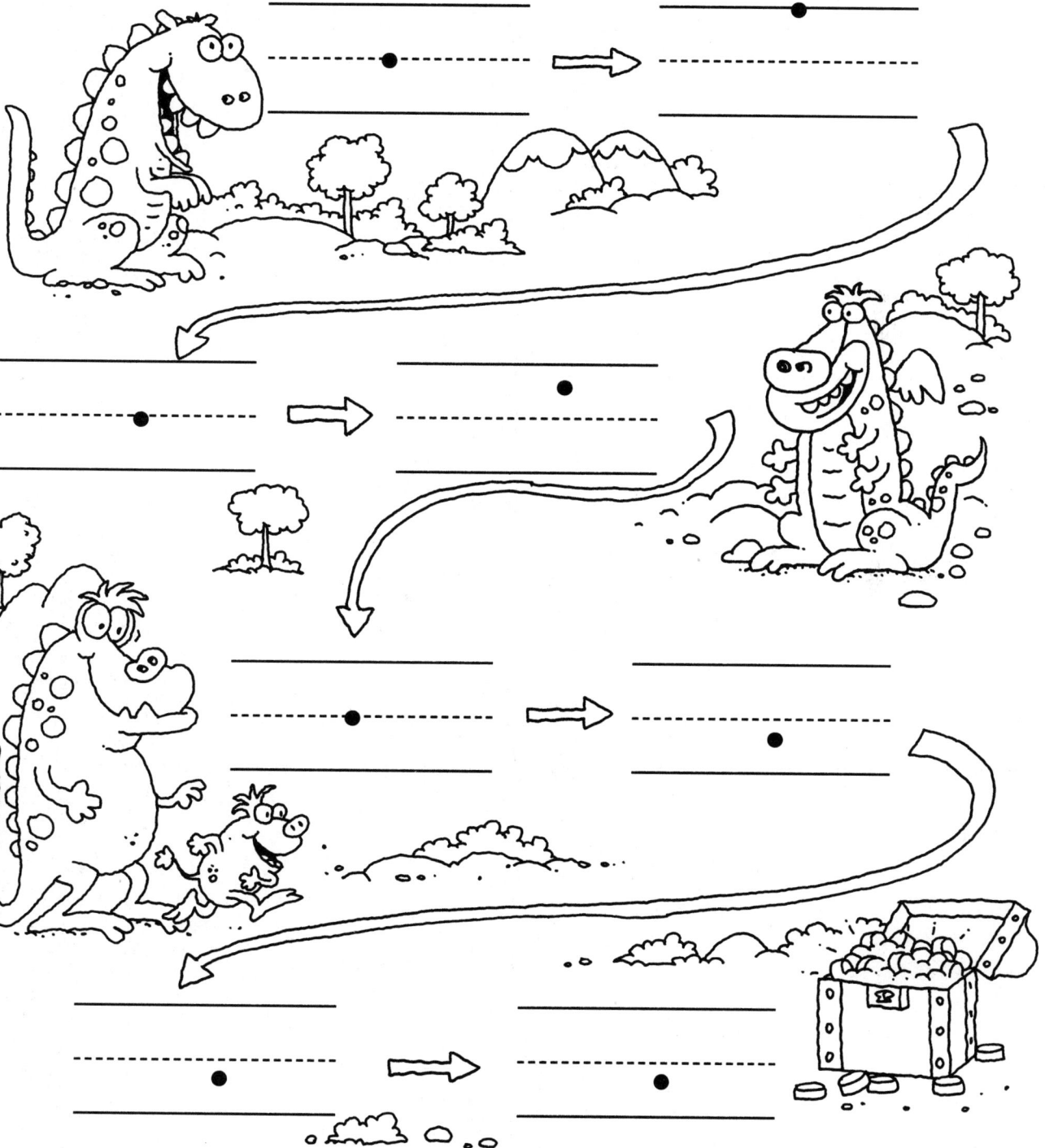

# Rhyme Time